THE COMMON MAN

Books by Maurice Manning

The
Common Man

MAURICE MANNING

HOUGHTON MIFFLIN HARCOURT

Boston   New York

2010

For information about permission to reproduce selections
from this book, write to Permissions, Houghton Mifflin Harcourt
Publishing Company, 215 Park Avenue South, New York, New York 10003.

www.hmhbooks.com

Library of Congress Cataloging-in-Publication Data
Manning, Maurice, date.
The common man : poems / Maurice Manning.
p. cm.
ISBN 978-0-547-24961-2
1. Appalachian Region — Poetry. I. Title.
PS3613.A5654C65 2010
811'.6 — dc22   2009029080

Book design by Patrick Barry
Text is set in Mercury

Printed in the United States of America

DOC 10 9 8 7 6 5 4 3 2 1

This book is dedicated to the memory

of my grandmothers, who told me stories,

and to the Kentucky mountains,

which made those stories happen.

CONTENTS

They were a man's words, a ballad of an old time

Sung among green blades, whistled atop a hill.

— JAMES STILL

THE COMMON MAN

MOONSHINE

The older boy said, Take ye a slash
o' this — hit'll make yore sticker peck out —

which would have been a more profound
effect than putting hair on my chest,

to which I was already accustomed.
Proverbially, of course, he was right.

I took a slash, another, and then
I felt an impassioned swelling, though

between my ears, as they say, a hot
illumination in my brain.

The shine had not been cut; full of
the moon it was for sure. I knew

the mountain county it came from —
my family's section, on Little Goose.

A distant cousin would have been proud
to know another cousin was drinking

what might as well be blood, at least
the bonds that come with blood, the laugh

before the tragic truth, the love
of certain women, the hate for lies,

the knowledge that death can be a mercy,
the vision blurred and burning there

1

in the mind and in the wounded heart.
This was the first time I heard the story

I was born to tell, the first I knew
that I was in the story, too.

THE MUTE

If you go up the holler far
enough you'll spy a little house

half-hidden in the trees. It's dark
up there all day and when the night

comes down it's darker yet. There's two
old brothers living in that house

and the younger one is fatter than
a tick with lies and sassy tales.

One time, a bear came through and ate
a couple dozen pawpaws these brothers

had shaken from the tree and left
lined up on the porch rail to ripen,

and Murdock, their good-for-nothing dog
who had retired to the porch on account

of all the work he'd done that day,
never so much as growled nor raised

an eye. The brothers were tending to
the pole beans in the garden patch

and once the bear had slunk away
both brothers said at once: Why, shoot

an' H-E-double-toothpicks, Murdock!
And then the younger one said: Jinx.

And the older brother spit in the dirt.
According to the younger one —

who couldn't hold his belly still
from all the laughter he'd provoked —

it was about a year and a half
before he let his brother speak,

but then it didn't last too long
on account of Murdock treed a woman.

She'd come up there to see how poor
these brothers were and if they needed

some religious reading material.
She called hello, then Murdock woofed

his woof as fierce as he could be,
and she shinnied up the pawpaw tree

and hollered: Help! Ole Murdock, well,
he never left the porch. The brothers

were digging a privy hole behind
the house and when the woman hollered,

they came running around and six feet off
the ground this pretty red-haired woman

was trembling in the pawpaw tree,
and the poor thing's skirt had gotten bunched

around her thighs as she was climbing up —
this otherwise respectable woman

came near to blinding the brothers right there,
her bloomers were so bright. Now, it took

a moment or two before the brothers
could gather their wits, but once they did

they tried to look concerned and turned
to the porch and said in a single voice:

You son-of-a-biscuit-eater, Murdock,
you've done scared this young gal halfway out of

her drawers! The younger brother grinned,
and jinxed the older one again.

Because I jinxed him! he told me one day
when I asked why I'd never heard

the older brother speak. How long
has he been jinxed? I asked. Lord, years!

he said, and I don't reckon he
remembers how to speak, and it's been

so long, I've plumb forgot his name;
I can't take back the jinx no more.

Now remember what I said — this man
is fatter than a junebug with lies

and he can spread them pretty thick,
though I've never minded listening.

Many a time I've stopped up there
to visit and every time it seems

the younger brother has just been waiting.
What's the good word? he always asks.

Yes, many a time I've stopped up there,
but I've never seen a pawpaw tree.

Lord knows what became of that young woman
or if she continued her ministry;

and one day ole Murdock went to Heaven —
why, even a bad dog gets to go.

A BESTIARY

The reason the woman was fond of chickens,
according to another woman

I overheard while mulling over
the scale with an ounce of turnip seed

hung in its craw — and whose opinion
was beyond dispute — the reason why?

Well, she was raised up with a rooster.
And that was that, the old nature

versus nurture debate resolved
in favor of the nurture, but let's

not leave the nature out. Clearly,
the woman came from people who knew

their child should be acquainted with
the big ideas, one of which,

that's right, is happiness, and roosters,
though prone to swings of mood and squabble,

are happy in the main. I knew
a woman raised up with a goat.

She couldn't read, but I don't think
it was related to the goat.

Though goats can sway a person, it's true,
and would rather eat a book than read it,

a goat won't hold you back. Were you
raised up with a beast beside you? I mean

a serious beast. Well, if you were,
you know you never owned it. Did

you ever give your thumb to a calf
and feel how hard it pulls, and feel

the pulling pull you? I don't care
if it has spurs or horns, a beast

will raise you up, and if you don't think
you need to be raised up, I'm afraid

it doesn't matter what you read;
you won't be happy, not in the way

that roosters are. I hate to be
the one to tell you, but even a girl

as poor as dirt will let her heart
be taken with a rooster, a cock

of the commonest walk, though you can crow
about it till the cows come home.

A WAVERING SPINDLE
OF FORSYTHIA

Well, I don't know if *spindle* is
the word; maybe it should be *stalk,*

but this is a thin one, it's freer,
and now its free end is hooping up

the air the way a boy who pulls
a stick from the fire to — what? — command

the night with the coal-tip, leaves
circles not quite completed, a line

not yet a shape but like one, like
a horseshoe, or the boy himself

about to ask it plainly, Why
do I like doing this? That boy,

he had a pony then, and rode it
around the dusty ring just once

before he slid the cribbed slat back
and swung the gate and left. We'll see,

he said, we'll see what happens now.
That night, in the company of stars

and, yes, the blessed pony, he made
the fire, and in a little while

he took the stick and drew the crown
of red around the pony's head.

THE PUPIL

Time was, I was there, halted beside
the drumstove. It glowed; there was

a skillet set on its head, biscuits
were rising on the coal-black brim.

I had a book and a full-grown woman
beside me. You might not believe it,

but I was teaching her to read.
Her father was in the other room;

he lay beneath a quilt to make
us think he was asleep. I could see

his boots still on his feet, pointing
at the sooty ceiling. He didn't want

his daughter to learn to read.
There was a hole in the roof and a cat

climbed through it into the stiff heat;
an ancient woman, who never spoke

and never noticed the cat, was strapped
to a chair with a belt — I had forgotten

the part about the cat and the belt
and the painted eyes of the woman. Why

was I until this moment afraid
to remember her? What kept her out? —

Now, the daughter didn't call her father
Daddy. Diddy, she said, Diddy,

git up! We got comp'ny. They's biscuits
comin', and besides I'm a-fixin' to read!

Why, even Granny wants to see,
don't you, Granny? She tapped her fingers

on the old woman's leather hand,
then shook her head and turned to me.

Dat Diddy's awful moody, she said,
and laughed. I peeked into the shadow

of his room. Her Diddy didn't flinch,
he didn't draw a breath. His boots

crowed like parentheses around
a word that had no letters, a space

where nothing held its place, a blank
for instance, a mute *as in.* What else

was there to do? That Diddy wasn't
any smarter than the handle

of a broom, yet still he knew. He knew
no book would help, no word would hold

him back from sleeping off the life
God gave him — biscuits, a hole in the roof,

a quilt to cover up his eyes,
a daughter who couldn't read her name.

A PRAYER TO GOD MY GOD IN A
TIME OF DESOLATION

I guess you know about it all,
my woman trouble. That's what I call it,

though in a way I should say the trouble
has been with you. It's pretty bad,

but tell me when was it pretty good?
I ain't complainin'. You like that *ain't*,

an uncouth *ain't* in a prayer to you?
He thinks he's tough now, don't he? No,

I'm gentle. If there's a rough old cob
round here, it's you, and I like you for it,

you sneaky old hidden son of a nothing.
Hey, do you remember what's her name?

She was such a little thing. She chirped
so perfectly I told her we

should live in a tree like a couple of birds.
It sure was fun to feel her flutter.

Is it okay to call it fun?
Because I liked it, though what I wanted

was what I thought the flutter should
have meant — a little time with you.

That was a stretch. Those were the days
when I believed you wanted me

to find a woman who wanted to live
in a tree, two birds of a feather,

all lovey-dovey. Well, it turns out
not many women want to live

in a tree, because not many women
think of themselves as birds. They're women,

people, and I don't get along
so well with people, thanks to you,

who bent my heart from the beginning
to creatures with four legs, or wings.

Have I told you you're a weirdo? You
should have made me a horse and been done with it;

I could have drawn a plow and scratched
my hide against a tree or cribbed

a fence in the pasture. Or better yet,
I could have been an owl and combed

the hair of night before she lays
her head to sleep. How's that for gentle?

I used to think it was you and me,
but now I think it's only you.

You're on your own, so be it. If that's
the way you want it, alone, amen.

THREE TRUTHS, ONE STORY

Well heck-o, Hoss, I can't make up
a name like Turnipseed! Or that

I knew a man who went by such
a goodly name. Now everything

I'm telling you is true. This man
had come from people who knew what they

were doing once, and why it mattered.
Do you know what you're doing? Do you

know something old? A turnipseed
is tiny, it's a little bit

of hardly anything. I guess
that's something old to know — you could hold

an itty bit of almost nothing
and know it's something still, and know

it's always been that way. Do you
like knowing things like that? I knew

a bunch of folks some years ago
whose name was Stonecypher — I kid

you not — and some of them were still
engaged with stones and had the hands

to prove it. They lived way out. Speaking
of out-there places, my father told me

just the other day, a tale
about his mother: Mama came

from Leatherwood, he said, Lord knows
what they were doing there, back then.

And that is true for sure, there's not
a living person left to say

what they were doing there. They had
a stripey mule, as Mama said —

the stripes run crossed the ginny's flank,
she told me once, but she is gone,

and missing her has gotten old.
There are words and there are deeds, and both

are dying out, dying away
from where they were and what they meant.

God save the man who has the heart
to think of anything more sad.

HEY, SIDEWINDER

You ready for a little fun?
Let's put the horse beside the cart

this time and see what happens. We won't
be getting ahead of ourselves

at all. We'll wait and tap along
with the drowsy bugs still twittering

from the darker reaches of the trees.
You hear? It's morning now, and not

a strain to see that horse and cart
beside themselves in the shady lane

that runs beside the barn. We know
already what the cart will do —

sit there, unmoved and unmovable,
a rough idea and just as useless,

temptation, we might could say, but not
the hell-for-certain tempter. Now,

there is a little bit of hell
to mention here — he's in the barn,

his clothes shucked off. But let's leave him
for the moment, naked in the shadows;

maybe he'll get a shiver! We've got
a horse to think about, and I

can tell you now he's not in the mood
to stand around all day. He prods

the ground with a hoof. Let's go! he says,
to the naked man (who's still in the barn

and halted for a second thought),
you hitch me up; if you're gonna do it,

let's do it now. Funny, that sounds
like a preacher I once heard — it's time

for the altar call! You see, this man
has killed another man to avenge

the honor of his wife, but has come
to discover that in fact his wife

took part in said dishonor and liked it,
and now the dead man's kin have sworn,

for what it's worth, to jerk a knot
in the tail of our naked man. I swear,

this is a complicated story.
Or is it? The naked man has secured

a dress and a bonnet belonging to
his wife who couldn't keep her legs

together, and who at present is naked
herself and tied fast to the post

of their sorry marriage bed. The horse
lets out a snort and works the bit

around in his mouth. He's waited long
enough, and steps in front of the cart

to make it easy for the man,
who now puts on the dress, severe

and long, and buttons up the back;
and once he ties the bonnet strings

he has this Granny Woman look,
as if he's off to bring a young'un

into the bright sunshiny day
with a slap across his little tater.

Now, friends, we know that slap
was just a tap from the buggy crop;

the horse stepped up and the cart rolled on,
and the man in woman's garb went with them.

It was a pretty good disguise,
all right, and don't you know, that man,

well, he delivered something — himself,
from a pointy-headed sheriff (who was

the brother of the deceased) and from
a dreadful marriage to a woman

who couldn't keep the holy bond.
A man's got a right to expect better

than that, and by golly, he got it,
with another woman, and pretty, too,

in another town, where they hadn't heard
of his earlier trouble. In time, they prospered,

and had a bunch of children, and one
of them was my own granny, born

a hundred years ago, or so,
when a woman kivered up her head —

well, that's the way she said it — and when
the dresses were a little longer

and, I'd say, more fun to remove, and when
we took a buggy ride or walked,

and when a man could count on a horse
to get him where he needed to go.

A BLASPHEMY

You wouldn't have believed it, how
the man, a little touched perhaps,

set his hands together and prayed
for happiness, yet not his own;

he meant his people, by which he meant
not people really, but trees and cows,

the dirty horses, dogs, the fox
who lived at the back of his place with her kits,

and the very night who settled down
to rock his place to sleep, the place

he tried so hard to tend he found
he mended fences in his sleep.

He said to the you above, who, let's
be honest, doesn't say too much,

I need you now up there to give
my people happiness, you let

them smile and know the reason; hear
my prayer, Old Yam. The you who's you

might laugh at that, and I agree,
it's funny to make a prayer like that,

the down-home words and yonder reach
of what he said. And calling God

the Elder Sweet Potato, shucks,
that's pretty funny, and kind of sad.

THE OLD CLODHOPPER'S AUBADE

I know two bluebirds tamed and flown
into a woman's eyes. She keeps

a country lit behind them, her eyes
I mean, and those bluebirds twine their song

around a hillside there. Lord God,
but it's a country, and guess who keeps

the shadow of it in his head?
Ole lonesome me! You see, one night —

you folks'll get a kick out of this —
I blew a little sunshine up

her skirt, and well, as far as I
could tell, she liked it. What can I say?

A man who knows the shadows knows
his way around the sunshine, too,

if you know what I mean. Now, I don't know
the story of how this woman taught

those birds to fly into her eyes,
and if I ever hear it, Lord,

she might not let me tell it! You see,
this woman is kind of funny — she asked

me once, after I'd told her how
she made me happy, What in the name

of God's own rooster do you know
about happiness? A widow's mite,

I said, but I know you have to wait,
and maybe wait some more. That ain't

nothin' to crow about, she said,
and the way you're callin' up the mornin',

I wisht you'd cut it out and sleep!
I can't cut out the morning, I said,

it's in my nature, my little chick-
a-dee with the bluebirds in her eyes.

Yore nature's strange, she said, and sighed.
Besides, my eyes ain't blue, they're green.

With that, she closed them tight, her eyes,
and the sun-ball hung his hat behind

the sky. The happiness I'd known
so little of had left a mark

to let me know I knew it less,
and, by God, that turned my nature dark.

ARS POETICA SHAGGY
AND BROWN

Tell me the story in your heart.
Does it involve a donkey? Does

the donkey have a name? I know
a donkey whose name is Clyde. I like

ole Clyde. When I walk to the patch
of cedars on the hill, I whistle,

and Clyde comes up from the barn he likes
to wait in. What's a-goin' on?

I say. Then Clyde swishes his tail
and looks me in the eye. I nod,

he nods, then both of us cock our ears
and look around. We wait and wait.

Most of the time there's nothing to hear,
nothing to notice, but a hawk

riding the last hot swell of the day
or a spider spinning. Well, tally-ho,

I say in a little while. He swishes
his tail again — Lord, I believe,

help thou my unbelief. Well, now,
he doesn't come out and say it, but that's

what he means by that easy swish. It looks
like a by-God moment to me. Maybe

you'd like to put ole Clyde in the story
in your heart; it would be all right, I guess.

Ole Clyde has seen it all. He saw
the old man hang himself in the barn.

He saw the rope the old man carried,
and watched the milk can topple over.

The old man gave one kick and that
was it. Well, there I go! I've put death

and God together again! Now all
I need is love. I guess it's there;

it always is, according to Clyde.
Right now, above my head I count

eleven dragonflies. You know
some people call them skeeterhawks?

You reckon I could ever run out
of stories in my heart to tell?

EMPTYING A RAIN GAUGE

One morning, I said it — Piss in a boot!
And I knew, as I shook two piddly drops

of water from the gauge, I'd become
all too familiar with disgust.

I didn't believe anymore in a world
that wouldn't let me measure it,

and so I became ironical,
right then and there. Let the record show

how sad and simple is that state
of mind, the domain of lazy bones

and standers by. Nobody wants
to hear it, but the world has a voice

behind it saying to anyone
in earshot, What are you gonna do?

That's evangelical, my friends,
in a worldly, not a churchly, sense,

and ministerial, because
every day something has to save the day —

or the days get lost and so do you.
A few days after my descent

into the hell of my own fancy,
my neighbor happened by. He said

he was cutting down young locust trees
and feeding the branches to his cattle.

He also claimed, in passing, to own
a twenty-five-pound rabbit. That's

a big'un, I said, and he said, Yep.
And there it was, a nip of Yep

to bring me back to the wondrous world,
and back to wondering about it —

it is a fundament, you know.
I couldn't rue another day

away; besides, I'd done the leaving.
And so I started over; rain

or no, the next morning I went outside
and said to that voice, Well, you tell me.

SOWING BUTTER BEANS
WITH A STICK

When these here beans get up they'll stand
a top hat higher than your head.

And fetching home a mess? Why all
you'll have to say is Howdy do

and they'll fall right in your basket. Shucks,
it mightn't hurt to slap a few

across your morning plate and see
if that won't make you feel as if

you'd died and gone up yonder way.
But it sounds like you have gone already,

before the first bean breaks the ground
with its curly little finger. Why,

just listen to yourself — all stretched out
and lazy — give a man a stick

and a poke of speckled beans, and sure
as the morning, he starts talking funny

and thinking of the afterlife,
believing he can taste it; for

a moment there, he thinks it's real —
though let's recall this man was in

a garden when he got transformed
and let's allow his back was bent

and in one hand he held a needle
and in the other hand a spool

of thread, and though it's true, he wasn't
really sewing, in a way, he was.

DEAD TREE, TWO CROWS, MORNING FOG

It's a hickory, the headless tree,
a pair of shaggy arms still raised

above the cedars circling
its waist. A drowsy, ragged throng

has gathered while the fog burns off.
Those arms look hoisted up and cinched

to stay in place forever, to say,
I am surrendering. Around

these parts it makes a graven image.
I know you're thinking now about

this tree, and maybe you're thinking why
is this man so bent on darkness? Well,

I'm not so bent. I like the tree,
and soon enough the sun will shine

it up and make it look more friendly.
Sometimes a tree looks like a sign

of something else, that's all I'm saying.
Besides, I didn't make the world

the way it is, so black and white
sometimes it's blinding. You'd think the fog

would want to cover up the tree,
but this morning it looked like a lifted veil.

Let's face it, in the world we know
we want what's hidden to pack more punch

than what's revealed — there's more than meets
the eye. I like that proverb, too,

but revelation damns the eye
or dooms it to admit, I see it. Now,

what is it? I told you what it is,
this time, a tree — that looks like a man

tied up, who's bowed his head. And so,
the pair of crows I've noted. When crows

close their eyes, do you know what they see?
A tree, they have a mind for the mind

of a tree. How very pantheistic!
I suppose it is, but can you think

of anything more true than the God
who goes on living in a tree?

A mercy branches out to find
whatever needs it, to make the thing

that needed mercy merciful —
the fog unto the tree, the tree

unto the crows, the crows unto
the part I'm going to tell you next.

If you've ever tried to mock a crow,
you know it ain't gonna happen, which makes

its foolery less foolish. One
lit out and landed on a horse.

The horse was almost white. You think
I had a say in what I saw?

The horse was happy to receive
the crow — that graven thing was over.

And by the way, it wasn't me
who put the echo in the woods

when the second crow forsook the tree
for another farther in the fog.

THUNDERBOLT, MY FOOT

This one's about half-crazy! It's got
a couple of bugs, a horse, a bunch

of history, a long preamble
on the two sides of memory,

and no telling what all else — so we'll skip
the invocation of the Muse.

Besides, I'm wound up tighter than
a clock and it's time to commence this tale!

You know that look an old man gets
when he's telling a story he's thought about

but never told before? His eyes
drop down, he even bends his stiff

old body over, because he's found
a rising split-rock spring, and there

he sees his boyhood face and all
the other world he lived in once

inside the glass on the other side
of the skeleton keyhole he's looking through;

and all the outside, inside world
is floating on that sunken pool

of water — the boy, the door, the prick
of light shot through the door, and the iris

of the young boy's steady eye gazing
from the smoky room inside the glass.

An old man looks back like that to tell
the story he was in, and to see

himself again inside it, but then
he stops because there's something there

he didn't know was there until
right now, and then he gets that look

I just went on and on about.
The very look my father got

one day after he asked me, Hey,
you wanna hear a dirty lim'rick?

and I knew he knew I'd answer yes,
and so I did. Let's see, he said,

and drew a breath: I went downstairs
to fetch a little cider and there

set a bedbug a-jackin' off
a spider, so I went back up

to fetch a little gin and the son
of a bitch was a-doin' it again!

He cackled, pleased that he'd remembered
it was a bedbug, not a skeeter,

though there is one about a skeeter. He said
he'd heard this limerick — which was less

a limerick than a bawdy scrap
of verse with higher aspirations —

he said he'd heard it late one night
in the old pool hall he hung around

when he was seventeen or so.
An old man told it, he said, seems like

he had a tune he sang it to,
but I can't remember how it goes.

His voice slowed down and trickled out,
and he bent over like a tree.

Guess what? He saw himself again,
back then in the story of the child

inside the memory of the man,
but the story wasn't going where

he thought it used to go, so he stopped.
Just hold on, friends! Because this tale

has more than bedbugs and spiders in it,
and things are fixing to take a turn.

Turns out, the man who sang this verse
was the grandson through his mother's side

of a famed, ill-tempered man they called
the Thunderbolt of the Confederacy.

I've seen his bronzy statue perched
atop his horse. A curious note

about this horse: she was a mare,
a mare horse named Black Bess —

a better name than Thunderbolt,
in my opinion. Now, I hate

to be indelicate about
such matters, but whoever made

this fancy statue didn't get
the horse part right, because not far

from the south end of this mare is a set
of monumental glands, about

the size of two big green tomatoes.
A curious note about the man

atop this most unusual mare:
my double-great-granddaddy, who

at the time was still a boy, caught him! —
he caught ole Thunderbolt one day

in 1864 and hauled
him to a Yankee prison. That day

was in my father's memory when
he told me the story of how he heard

the dirty limerick; even the past
he wasn't part of was in the glass,

because the past was part of him
and now, a lifetime later, he saw it,

and now I saw it, too. Of course,
only part of this story gets

resolved, but it's pretty good from here
on out. I asked if the grandson was fit

to be the heir to a Thunderbolt.
Hah! Thunderbolt, my foot, was how

my father answered: The grandson drank
and gambled, and he was bad at both.

He drank his life away, I guess,
which was sad to see, but I shook him for

a little of his money — that night
we played some nine-ball and, uh, well,

I ran the table seven times.
I took all the foldin' money he had;

reckon I took his little lim'rick, too.
But then he got that look again;

the glass held something else, beyond
his past, sired by the story told

to the dam of memory, the issue of
that past — a later past to come.

Well, friends, ole Thunderbolt was trouble,
he stole and killed, he even escaped

that Yankee prison, but in the end
he found a bullet in Tennessee.

I guess some folks would say that's justice,
but I'd say the dishonor done his horse

and the shame that came his grandson's way,
that's something more, that's poetry.

THE BURTHEN OF THE
MYSTERY INDEED

Let's think about the landscape now
where all of this is happening,

the work-worn shoulder of the hill,
the brush of trees above like hair

uncaught by a hat brim, the sky
of unknown mind, the deafened head

inside the salty hat, and across
the darkened skin of naked neck

a line of muddy cows. Let's say
the line is muddy, too, because

it's far enough away for you
to see it vaguely. There's nothing else

to say about this scene, too wrought
perhaps, too willfully described,

implying love and tragedy
at once. There is no center point,

no frame to hold it still, but you
are in the landscape, too. I need

to know if you are shamed or glad,
if this is doom or grace, because

I know the terrible side of you
would burn it all if you could, this spot

of time outside of time, this place
of too much kindness for your kind.

A PANEGYRIC AGAINST THE
CONSOLATION OF GRIEF

Yes, my heart is sore and heavy-laden,
as if it's pulled too much too long,

and in our especial rural scene,
as someone called it once, that puts

the heart in the company of a team
of mules, or going farther back,

to a single ox, who's burdened by
a question for the heartless man

behind him: why cut down the tree
that gives you summer shade? Of course,

the ox knows the man enough to know
he doesn't have an answer. Meanwhile,

the man is applying a switch to the back
of the ox who's struggling to haul

the log out of the woods — and all
the ox can say? Well, I'll be damned.

That's what I mean by grief, and why
it shouldn't be consoled; it hides

a deeper, unanswerable grief
and where it comes from. What the hell's

a panegyric anyway?
Some pretty praise, a speech. We've had

enough of those, especially
on the rural scene — the field at dusk,

a dog and a man admiring it.
Besides, that scene is fading out,

little by little it's being felled,
all felled, and it won't be coming back.

Can anyone among you say
you've had the pleasure of knowing an ox?

Or a tree? Or the water in a spring?
I'm getting preachy now. I'm sorry.

But let me say sometimes a grief
is all you've got, and so you keep it

to remember what you loved and know
what loved you back, and it might come down

to a tree or a field. If a man tells you
his truest friend in the whole wide world

was a dog, the best that ever was,
believe him, then leave him alone. He's sad,

but sadder for his scene; the God
who made it only made it once.

A WRINGER WASHER
ON THE PORCH

Now it's not the eyesore you might think;
there's plenty of reasons why a porch

is just the place for a wringer washer.
I know a possum who lived in the tub

of one, one winter, and a boy
I know, well, let's just say he hung

his coat in a funny place that year.
Some folks don't have too many clothes,

which simplifies their lives. A man
might have two pair of britches to

his name; a woman, one black dress
for funerals and something less

fancy for all the other days,
and — and this is the real humdinger of

the romantical tale I'm fixing to tell —
an apron: you know the kind I mean,

the kind with strings the woman ties
without a peek behind her back.

There was a man around these parts
who lived alone and, according to

a number of his neighbors, was not
well practiced in domestic arts,

which is to say, this fellow kept
a wringer washer on his porch,

and as far as anyone could tell,
seldom was the washer put to

its intended purpose, and, in fact,
was just the size to accommodate

the recipe this uncouth man
had concocted to make a batch of wine —

it was summer, blackberry time.
Enter now a woman, a bit

high-strung some say, who'd lately joined
the local temperance league and thus

had been appointed to apprise
this man of all his wickedness.

What followed next remains unclear,
but it's apparent that the man

did not take kindly to the wrath
of a woman he didn't even know

and her judgments about what he kept on his porch.
Some sort of scuffle soon broke out

and in the confusion the strings that held
the woman's apron around her waist

got wound up in the wringer somehow.
She was stuck like a fly to a tape, and the man,

a little pleased I guess, sat down
on an old nail keg. He might have scratched

himself, for all I know, in a place
that, shall we say, would have offended

a lady's sensibilities.
The story goes, she began to holler,

and the more she hollered, the madder she got,
until pretty soon she was cussing him.

About the time the moon came up,
the woman grew hoarse, and hushed. The man

took a look at the moonlight on her hair
and smiled. You know what I reckon, he said,

you're twiced as intemp'rant as me, Sister.
Well, you can probably figure out

what happened next — they laughed, and then
he convinced her that a little wine

might soothe her throat and he was right,
it did, so she had a little more,

and before she knew it, she was soothed
all over and was kind of glad she'd got

wound up to that wringer after all,
and, by gum, hit was one hell of a porch

they was a-dancin' on! — I forgot
to tell you, after a while the man

and woman started dancing. He took
the handle of the wringer and wound

her out to him and wound her back.
The crickets must have chirped the tune.

Remember the boy who hung his coat
in the washer tub? Well, he was born,

all right, about a year later;
the possum didn't live there yet.

FOR THE LAST TIME, NO, I'M
NOT THE RABBIT MAN

But I happen to know the man they call
the Rabbit Man, and it's a fact,

he's known by his persuasion. Why, he's got
more rabbits than sense, and they've all got names

from the books of the Good Book and because
there's more rabbits than books he's doubled up,

so there's a fat rabbit he calls
Ecclesiastes the Second, and such

as that. And that's the Rabbit Man —
he's got a crooked back, and if

the man can walk from there to here
in a straight line, I've never seen it.

But he's all right. Now, he's got a sister;
she's married up, he says, to a man

who's more than twiced her age, and she
fell in with him because she learned

he'd raised a whippoorwill from its egg,
and then the durned thing wouldn't leave

and she just had to see that bird
he kept in an apple crate as big

as you please. And thus, according to
the Rabbit Man, it pleased his sister

to see this whippoorwill, so she
kept going back to see it. Well,

it wasn't long before she took
a notion she had to hear it sing,

which meant she had to stay until
the dew had fallen at least — and by then,

it wasn't ladylike for her
to be there, in that dark house with that

old man, and nothing but a bird
to make him mind his manners. So,

pretty soon they wound up married,
this sister of the Rabbit Man

and her gentle husband who was born
no telling how many years ago.

Now listen, I know this all sounds strange,
but it happens. A person gets a spark

from the way another person lives
and what's so wrong with that? People

come by here all the time, and all
the time they've got a question. Are you

the Turtle Man? You wouldn't be
the Chicken Man? I tell them no.

A woman came by not long ago —
she was so pretty I had to stare

at her feet, which was good and bad because
she wasn't wearing any shoes.

She pointed a toe and wondered if
I was the Redbone Man. Now, what

she wanted with a redbone hound
I'll never know, but I can tell you,

you've never seen such hesitation
overcome a man. Yet I looked up

and said, No ma'am. And then I could see
the disappointment in her eyes,

heck, I was disappointed, too.
A barefoot woman at my door,

imagine that! Imagine how
my homely threshold heaped up like

a grave between us there, a long
neglected spot, and both of us

bewildered by our hem and haw,
too spooked to take a step across it.

—

THAT DURNED OLE
VIA NEGATIVA

You ever say a word like *naw,*
that *n, a, double-u* instead

of *no*? Let's try it, *naw.* You feel
your jaw drop farther down and hang;

you say it slower, don't you, as if
a *naw* weighs twice as much as *no.*

It's also sadder sounding than
a *no.* Yore Daddy still alive?

a friend you haven't seen might ask.
If you say *naw,* it means you still

cannot get over him. But would
you want to? *Naw.* Did you hear it then,

that affirmation? You can't say *naw*
without the trickle of a smile.

The eggheads call that wistful, now —
O sad desire, O boiling pot

of melancholy pitch! Down in
that gloomy sadness always is

a hope. You gittin' any strange?
That always gets a *naw,* and a laugh.

I've had that asked of me. It's sad
to contemplate sometimes, but kind

of funny, too. It makes me think
of *git* and who came up with that,

and the last burdened letter hitched
to *naw,* that team of *you*s and yoked

together — the you you are for now
and the you you might become if you

said yeah, to feel the sag of doubt
when only one of you is left

to pull the load of living. My,
but we're in lonesome country now.

I wonder if we ever leave it?
We could say yeah, but wouldn't we

be wiser if we stuck it out
with naw, and know the weight of what

we know is dragging right behind us,
the squeak and buck of gear along

with us, O mournful plea, O song
we know, by heart, by God, by heart.

THE LORD HE THOUGHT
HE'D MAKE A MAN

You know those bones are bound to rise —
no doubt about it, even the bones

of a bad man rise, even the bones
of your own voice singing rise,

though it's easy to think they won't. They lay
unsung for years and then one day

you're all grown up with a pack of sorrows
and you start humming something strange,

and it all makes sense, the coming back
of the past and what we're calling bones —

and there's bones aplenty. Remember the song
about the fox and the chilly night?

Well, he goes out all right and what's
he got when he comes back? A goose,

and pretty soon he's cooked it up
and the little ones are suckin' on

the bones-o, bones-o. Remember what
Aunt Rhodie's waiting for? The death

of her old gray goose so she can get
a good night's sleep. That's two dead geese

by my count and it just gets worse. When she —
whoever the hell she is — comes round

the mountain, all the folks will be
so glad, they'll kill the old red rooster!

She must have been a prodigal
of sorts. It doesn't matter where

she's been or how she got the money
to buy those six white horses, nope,

she's coming back and everything
will be right as rain when she comes round.

Unless you're the rooster. It hurt to sing
the song back then; you wanted to save

that rooster and put him in the barnyard
of another song, and now, when those bones

have come back red and sad, it hurts
again and maybe more, because

you see your life has been one sorrow
after another and still you love it

like a child who knows no better. You want
your bones to rise but only if

you get to take the sorrow, too.
Now why is that? Because there is

another song you used to sing.
This man gives his love a cherry without

a stone and a chicken without a bone
and a story that never ends and a baby

who never cries. It's what they call
a riddle song. It riddled all

the others because it was happy
and sad at once. It seemed to be

a song about another place,
the place where you were born and raised

the first go-round, and when you rise
again you hope it happens there.

FOR THE PRODIGAL, THE MORNING IS
A TRESPASS AGAINST THE NIGHT

In dissipation, friends — and let's rub
our hands together thoughtfully

for this solemn moment — there clings a drop
of wisdom, wouldn't you agree?

Not that I'd advocate a life
of carrying on with the tipple swill

or ill-reputed women, but
the morning after a tipper, say,

the feeling is bad, you feel your life
is draining out and you alone

are hastening the lonely swirl
to nothingness. And then the shame

commences. Lord, I am a sinner,
you rasp, now what in tarnation got in

to me last night? The blinding hooch,
for one, as if we need an answer.

The darker question is what got in
with being born, what followed you

from God's old brain? Ain't rubbin' our hands
together now! My, how the sweet thrill

sours down. Aren't you ashamed sometimes
to be alive? Now, that's a wallop —

and a mite unfair, so let's back up
to a colorful tale from days gone by,

and then we'll see how things turn out.
I knew a feller when I was young

who told me about a morphodite
he'd seen at the fair when he was a boy.

A dollar got you in the tent,
another dollar fetched a peek

at what he called her booger: she had
a little pecker up in thar

about yea-long, he said, and ran
his thumb across his finger, and grinned

to see me scared and wondrous. Half
the time this man lay broken down

and drunk, but when he wasn't drunk
he lived for the Lord alone. Now, it took

a while — there was a time of back
and forth, and the back was bad: his wife

gave up and left, he got his teeth
knocked out by a crazy woman who'd stuffed

a hambone in her stocking toe
and slung it at his head, and his son

got thrown in jail for something or other —
but eventually, he gave up. He said,

The Lord has fixed me for good this time
'cause I weren't aimin' to fix myself,

and as far as I could tell, it stuck:
he never took another drop;

he found another wife, he got
some teeth somewhere, and his son shaped up.

He'd fought the Devil and with some help
he'd won, and guess what? He laughed about it!

So, now you see where we've arrived;
it's bitter morning after — what?

And isn't that a funny question?
What happened? What got in to you,

and what has been there longer than
your twirling name? You could say nothing,

and in a way it would be true —
the original sin of sin is sin —

though it's just another way to say
I wish the Lord would fix me, too.

OLD NEGRO SPIRITUAL

They ain't no freedom. What man be free
from the air him breathe, or set a-loose

from the ground what's under his two feets?
It ain't a man nor woman borned

a-bein' free! That's what the man
was telling me. He had a name

that might make you laugh awkwardly,
because it's hard to believe: Catfish.

Ole Cat sho need a drank, unh huh,
him need a drank, all right, he'd said,

and coughed. It sounded like his voice
came out of a hole, from underground

and deep. I said I hoped he'd free
himself from the whiskey one day. I've told

you what he said to that, and when
he said it — not as a preacher might,

but as a man whose troubled heart
was sad for every one of us —

I nodded. He was right. And so,
by hook and crook in our dry county,

we wound up with a bottle, late
one late October night. Him know,

he said, if they be any thang
what's true, ole Cat gon' have to wait —

and you gon' do some waitin', too.
I'd met him in the stripping room.

He sang the oldest songs of all,
and in between he'd tell me what

a woman likes. They's ones what is
par-tickler, he said, and blew

the tobacco dust away from him.
He had a crippled dog named Dog.

Ole Dog him like dat Cat, he said,
as if he wasn't really there,

when we were well into the bottle
and Dog had given him a wink.

Has God forsaken anyone?
Well, yes and no. It depends, I guess.

Ole Cat descended one winter. Dog
outlived him, but he missed that Cat.

This really happened, long ago,
when I had more hope than I do now,

but I remember being there
and sometimes it causes me to tremble.

So there you have it, a white man
remembering an old black man,

remembering his voice, the way
it sounded, a song inside the sound;

it hurt to hear it then, and it hurts
that I can't hear it anymore.

O STATIONERS!

You people don't know the half of it!
How many words are gone forever,

no syllable or sound remains;
how many stories die on the lips

of the teller? What diversity
of meter never mattered, what

old numbers never made your list?
And what will not be entered on

this date or any other ever?
The story of two boys who stole

a horse and rode it all the way
to Gloryland, and one of them

was barefoot and cried a little bit?
What could the other boy have said

to make the barefoot boy all right,
if anything? There must have been

a fable way back when, about
a spider and a wren: the bird

has a broken leg, but the spider spins
a tiny splint because the wren

has promised to teach the spider how
to sing, which actually happens; though

the wren retains a permanent limp,
the two of them become old friends

and, yes, sometimes they weave and spin
from being drunk on happiness.

Would anyone of your Company
subscribe to that? Would anyone

agree to print a vulgar verse
my father said to me — I had

a little chick that wouldn't lay
an egg, so I poured hot water up

and down her leg. The li'l chick cried
and the li'l chick begged, then the li'l chick laid

me a hard-boiled egg. Is that
not terrible and beautiful

at once? I tell you when I heard it
as a boy, it made me want to get

a chicken; it made me feel my father
had thrown a book against my head.

A LEXICON FOR PEOPLE WHO
DON'T TALK TOO MUCH

Does anyone still say he runs
a right smart cattle? Does anyone

believe the man who's pucker-mouthed
and runs those cows is doing right

or being smart? If you have heard
his whoop or watched his dewlap quiver,

if you are ready to accept
a holler and watch the cows become

a lowing line that moves from hill
to bottomland and breaks itself

to silent dots before the moon
reweaves the field as Heaven's cloth;

if you cannot escape the fact
that cloth is finely woven, then you

will never doubt that the woman who says
she's bound for yonder when the day

arrives will make the river glad
when she tests it with her baby toe

and strides across it; or that her wake
will be remembered by the river

as a joy, the likes of which would be
untelling if it ever was

before, but sure to be back then
when God was just a little thing,

the river just a bitty trickle,
and all things in the main were small.

OLD-TIME PREACHIN' ON A
SCRIPTURE TAKEN FROM A TREE

A mind unhitched to a heart? — Shuckies!
If a mind don't drag a heart behind it

like a pony cart, I say, what kind
of mind is that, but wandered off,

and not just astray, a-lost! That heart
is like a tree cut from its roots —

a sip of freedom, spiked with the gall
of death, a breathing in without

the chance to let it go. That's what
a theory is, my friends, 'taint real,

it's rootless and unrooted in time,
and also meaning. Yes, *to mean*

means not just now, but all the way
to yonder. A good idea is good

because it begs a spell to reach.
Now, a tree will not deny its roots

and roots will not betray the ground
they're woven to, and none of it

will say there's no such thing as sun
or wind or rain. That makes a heap

of hearts hitched up to trees. Now ask
yourself which is more free, a tree

or you, and which of the two gives freely?
By grabbies, what's true for trees is true

for mountains, rivers, birds — gracious!
This is where you're livin' and everything

you love is here! Now ain't that
a pleasant breeze, and ain't that

a lovely rustle in the leaves?
To hear it is to hear ourselves

belonging where we live, and blessed.
But let's not think together we

have found this perty thing; let's know
it is the other way around:

we're found and made and rooted here,
and bound to being where we're bound.

I hope we're going to the heart,
I hope we're tied up in that glory.

Oh, recall that hilltop sermon and all
those blessings flowing from it for

the meek and poor, them other folks
half-whipped. If you can see where such

a river winds right down to you —
you salt and pepper of this earth —

then look up and pinch your eyes to see
just where that river got its start:

you'd best believe that mount is real
and where we always are forever.

Let us think about that with our hearts,
beating in amen time. Amen.

PAPPY'S LITTLE PISTOL

My Daddy, the sometime king of rage
and mourning, was resolved. I've done heard

the black shroud flappin' on the line,
he said. Some angel's washed it up

and hung it out: it's got my name
upon it, son, and it won't be long

before I wear it. I nodded, not
because I wanted to, but because

the old man's always had a way
of ruling out dispute — as when,

in my twelfth year or so, he delivered
his single-sentence homily

on women — Don't ever sleep with one
you ain't a-willin' to marry. Not

a claim on behalf of virtue, now is it?
Yet I've had to think about it a time

or two, and that might be all he wanted.
And now he wanted something else,

something he'd connived and dreamed about.
But I don't want nary a stitch on me

when that damned ole undertaker lays
me in the box, he said. Nekkid

as the first light of the morning is how
I'm going out. He grinned like a possum.

Okay, I said, I guess even
an ornery cuss like you deserves

a farewell do-si-do. Now I
was grinning, too, but then the sparkle

in his eyes dimmed down. I ain't done, yit,
he said. I want you to load the shotgun

and lay it with me in the box
and hook my finger on the trigger.

What makes you think you need a shotgun
in Heaven, and loaded, too? I asked.

'Cause I ain't goin' to Heaven first.
Before I cross the bar I aim

to bust my Pappy out of Hell —
he was one murderin' son of a gun

and never got the chance to be
redeemed, so I'm goin' down to bring

him back. No one was grinning now.
Don't you believe in God and that stuff

about the final mercy? I asked.
Hell, yes, he said, but sometimes the Lord's

a little slow, and the Devil got
my Pappy first; he didn't have

no other way to turn but mean.
He stopped and looked upon the hills

and hollers. We were at the homestead,
the place where everything that happened

had come to rest. A summer morning
on the porch, the fog was burning off,

the springhouse burbled and sounded like
a horse hitched to a beam and turning

a wheel — what wheel could it have been
but my defeat? My father said,

I had a happy childhood here;
I wish you could have had it, too.

I didn't nod this time. He knew.
Now I don't know if I believe

the Devil's faster than the Lord,
but I hope they write it down in Heaven

the day a toothless hillbilly
wakes up buck-naked and blasts the doors

of Hell right off their hinges to fetch
his outlaw Pappy from the fire.

I'd say there'd be commotion down
below, and jubilation yonder.

SAD AND ALONE

Well, this is nothing new, nothing
to rattle the rafters in the noggin,

this moment of remembering
and its kissing cousin, the waking dream.

I wonder if I'll remember it?
I've had a vision of a woman

reclining underneath a tree:
she's about half-naked and little by little

I'm sprinkling her burial mounds
with grass. This is the kind of work

I like. It lets me remember, and so
I do. I remember the time I laid

my homemade banjo in the fire
and let it burn. There was nothing else

to burn and the house was cold;
the cigar box curled inside the flames.

But the burst of heat was over soon,
and once the little roar was done,

I could hear the raindrops plopping up
the buckets and kettles, scattered out

like little ponds around the room.
It was night and I was a boy, alone

and left to listen to that old music.
I liked it. I've liked it ever since.

I loved the helpless people I loved.
That's what a little boy will do,

but a grown man will turn it all
to sadness and let it soak his heart

until he wrings it out and dreams
about another kind of love,

some afternoon beneath a tree.
Burial mounds — that's hilarious.

A LOCAL YOKEL'S SYSTEM
OF THE SPHERES

Aw, heck, let's take the longer way
around the barn, what do you say?

Let's say our little loop will lead us,
as usual, to the short end of

the stick; but the shorter end's the one
we want, because, by Jiminy Christmas,

it fits across our hand. But wait:
before we close our circuit, let's talk

about our stretched-out way around,
a path that makes the way so doomed

and dark, it becomes the only way.
You could wake up in the moonlight drunk

and sneak a peek up Heaven's skirt,
and in the morning you'd know for sure

you had a revelation, but
you can't remember how it went!

Now, it's easy to see the barn is the center
of our simple universe — well made;

how well it stands against the sag
of time, and how good it is the barn

is pulling us around it — fine.
We can also contemplate the hue

of the barn and how it matches the hue
of winter sky, as well as the lot

beside the barn. You see? We've got
three sorely dun-draped planes before us.

I suppose they meet along some line
of points to form an axle, which puts us

somewhere, amid the hum of a gray
enormous wheel. The wheel of what?

Good question! And hell if I know the answer.
That's why we'd better reach for our friend,

the stick, and its amended end.
I say we make a whistle from it

and see where it gets us. Pucker up
and give us a yee-haw tune, like "Dixie" —

now there's a ditty for the days
when everyone was itchin' to pick

a little cotton! Or try your hand
at the "Battle Hymn," that march of pride

in knowing right is on the side
of might and God is with us, too.

P-shaw, I don't think the Old Bird cares
for might, not ours. What about another one

from the olden days, say, "Wayfaring Stranger"?
It doesn't put us in a line

to anywhere, no way-back-when,
no one-day-soon, but doesn't that suit

our homespun loop? We're going around;
there's a short way and a long way, but

they're pretty much the same, and by God
we're poor and lost without the barn,

that comedy of gray! — which might
as well be empty on the inside,

though it's really stuffed to the gills with hay.
Now, you'll need your little whistle stick;

if you can whistle good, it helps
to keep from feeling lonesome. The ground

we're standing on is gray, the sky
is gray, the barn is also gray;

and God is grayer than a mule,
and about a hundred times as stubborn,

if you want to know the truth. Truth is,
we have no choice. I've been around

the barn alone before and seen
a shadow swinging in the shade

and wondered, Lord, has someone gone
and killed himself again? And then

I saw the shadow was the shape
of a leaf belonging to a tree

I couldn't see, and it made me mad.
What else is going on around

this barn? I shouted. Don't tell me
the wilderness is gone — I've seen it!

And I also know what Heaven is —
a garden with a tree that won't

burn up, a tater bug or two,
and a crow who goes by the name of You.

THE DOCTRINE OF AN AX

Of all times, now is not the time,
given the world's old vague condition,

to hang in my mind the plumb-bob pitch
of original sin and watch it twist

around like a tire at the end of a rope
looped over a tree branch. Once

my sister came within a hair
of getting bit by a snake asleep

in the tire she'd hooped around herself.
She was wearing a dress, my friends, just home

from church, her patent leather shoes
kicked at the air just twice before

she shed the tire and screamed. I chopped
the copperhead to pieces. What kind

of parents allow their child to play
with an ax? Well, mine, I suppose. I made

them proud that day. The sin was how
I let myself be proud, a pride

that wore like whitewash from a fence.
Now you might think I'm being stern

and unforgiving. After all,
I was only six and could not have known

about sin. But I did; I knew it like
a nursery rhyme, or the "Now I Lay Me"

bedtime prayer. I once got drunk
on a Sunday morning; I don't know

if that was sinful, but it proved
that nothingness is absolute,

a naked shameful nothing left
beneath the shade tree in my heart,

the rusted ax head long since stuck
and buried in its trunk, a bone

caught in its living throat, a wound
I made in its side and can't undo.

I should be doing something good,
I should be kind to someone now.

THE MAN WHO LIVED WITH JOY
AND PAIN: HIS OWN ACCOUNT

Suppose you were a farrier,
a man designed to hammer shoes

on horses' hooves, and you were good
enough that all you had to do

was listen to a horse's walk —
the *clip* is right, but the *clop* is off,

you'd say, a hand rung round your ear,
to tell the shoe was shoddy. Well,

one day, this horse comes in and, sure
as you're sitting there, the *clop* of the right

front hoof bespeaks instead a *clump*.
I need another, Brother, says

the horse. The *clop*'s went outta this'un.
You pull the old shoe off and rasp

the hoof to make it pretty, give
the new shoe a ping or two

until it fits. And just before
you drive the first nail home, the horse

says, Whoa! You'd better use the big'uns —
and turns his head to a bucket full

of railroad spikes. You're gonna need
a bigger hammer, friend, he snorts,

lifting the hoof like a mirror, just
the size of your face. We must remind

ourselves how rare it is to hear
a talking horse, and rarer still

to listen, how hard it is to keep
an iron belief from swinging down.

SONG OF THE POTATO DIGGER

Potatoes like me, they do. They know
I'm quiet in their rows, which lets

them better hear the silver song
of my gooseneck hoe, although I am

undoing some of them each time
the hoe comes down to sound its note.

I bank the open wound with dirt;
and if a dram of sweat rolls off

my chin, the potatoes think I'm weeping
at my task. And in a way, I am.

This work is often bitter, I tell you,
but can you think of anything

that's good that doesn't come from salt?
Can you imagine a man whose views

are more boiled down than mine, a man
who isn't cursed so much as bound

to think about his work? I can't.
But that's all right. I'm limited;

I break the heart of every day
I tuck a stone in my pocket and walk

outside to hang the hoe across
my shoulder like a lamb. And then

I heal the day as best I can
by bending gladly over it;

I make a long apology,
a necessary song, before

I straighten up and sweep my face
goodbye. Forget me for the night,

I say, to anyone who's left
to listen. My hilly world is sweet.

Love is grim. Sometimes I stoop
and eat it as I would a breath.

A MAN WITH A ROOSTER
IN HIS DREAM

All right, I'll tell you the weirdo dream
I had, but before I unwind that yarn,

let's twist our common thread. Like you,
I stare plumb through the wall sometimes,

because I'm thinking of a tree
and a little tenant house beside it,

and you-know-who on the stone step watching
as I pretend I'm a butterfly

and beg the flowers pretty please
to open wider for the bees.

That old communion scene won't go
to sleep, and I hope we both agree

it shouldn't. Now, about that dream.
I was just a tadpole, eight or nine,

so yonder down the road from home
that when a storm had pinched the sky

into a fist and looked to shake it,
I was afraid I might get drowned or struck,

so I ran up on this widow's porch
and in the flash I saw her. She held

a hatchet in one hand and spanked its head
against her other palm. Thar, thar,

she said, hit's just a little thunder,
and cocked her head. In the corner I saw

the comb of a one-legged rooster,
bristled and bobbing up and down.

Sometime he turn so troublesome
and mean, I chop his little laig off

to set him straight, but then that laig
grows back, so I chop it off again!

She cackled and pulled the porch-light string,
and pointed with the hatchet handle

to a bucket full of rooster feet,
their spurs still sharp, but clumped together

like rusty nails, and beyond the bucket
I caught the red-eyed glare of the rooster,

who hopped in place a couple of times
as if to punctuate his position.

Hit's like the devil with that rooster,
the widow woman said, around

and around — good gracious — and even when
he's down to just one bony laig

he don't set still! — You wouldn't want
a peg-leg rooster would you, boy?

That was the last the widow said.
Did I run home? Did a fist of rain

beat down on me that night; did I tuck
that rooster underneath my arm?

I could have given him a name,
or watched his little leg grow back,

poor thing, or looked him in his eye
to see if something really real

was hiding in the bloodshot room
behind it. Now, does he belong

in that communion scene with the bees
and butterflies, that honeyed day

in spring that never has a midnight?
I'm afraid he does. In fact, I think

that pretty bird is always perched
in the blown-down shadow of the tree

I make each magic night when I see
the face of love in her doorway lit

by the moon, and she draws me in. And then
I see she's staring not quite at me

but at some whimsy in the grass.
She loves that rooster more than me —

well, that's what I think, when she clenches her teeth
because that gritty word is tied

like a clover button to her tongue
and she can't decide if she should spit

or bite it into smaller words.
That's the gaze we always face,

in dreams and otherwise — the slate
of mischief mocking, mocking hope,

the imperfections of the tree,
the privations of the tenant house —

who dreamed this country hoedown up? —
the one-armed clock God's handyman

has nailed to the wall of the endless day
and wound up with a key, a key!

THE BEET'S THEOLOGY

By God, the leaves are frilly things,
though pretty near to naked — you

can see the blood right through the veins!
So comes the beet into the world:

its hat pops up a little like
the stovepipe type of yore, more hat

than head. But that's all right, it gives
the beet more room to think, and when

you sit in a row all day you feel
inclined to stretch the old hat rack out —

Well, well, the season is short and long
enough. I've had my lot of earth,

my share of rain and summer dew.
I could have stood some more. Too bad

a she-beet never called me hither,
but I suppose I couldn't have gone,

since, sad to say, I haven't got
a leg to stand on much less to go

wherever hither lies! It would take
a miracle to get me there —

And there you have the beet's dilemma,
the faith and deeds routine won't fit.

All a beet can do is wait,
and even if the hand of Heaven

should pluck it out, it might not know.
Is that theology or no?

OH, SHE'S WARM!

If you're like me, you know them well —
the winter tales — the night it turned

so cold the moon got stuck in the sky,
and in the morning some hero type

with a long-handled ax and ladder chopped
it out, which let the world get back

on track; or the year the rooster's tongue
got frozen to his upper beak,

and were it not for the boy who held
a match beneath the rooster's chin,

no telling who would still be sleeping.
Now these are funnies, but let's agree

they're a tad bit implausible.
Whole families freeze to death, and the reason

they don't wake up is unrelated
to the moon or a tongue-tied rooster.

I happen to know a little wren
who didn't eat for days until

I had the gall to feed her, because
some pair of hands had worked the loom

of the season to weave a shawl of ice
so thick, it covered every seed

and undropped berry of the field,
so help me God. You probably know

the kind of field I'm talking about —
that kind of beauty keeps us out,

or on the edge, but the wren was in it
and came out of it to me, and ate

a crumbled biscuit from my hand.
And I was moved to laughter. Strange.

I realize this isn't much of a tale;
it isn't very funny, but

it's true, and I'm sick of those folksy yarns
whose creatures tough it out, whose moral

is to get up in the morning and do
what must be done without complaint.

We have to do that every morning;
there's no moral to it. But the wren

did something else: she broke the glass
of what I thought was beautiful,

and then she broke the satisfaction
I'd taken from the winter scene

and made me laugh, which lessened the sting.
I'd been so wrong and so glad about it.

Since then, I've got a little saying:
you never know when you'll need a biscuit.

Now, the moral here is the Devil hates
surprises; he's a flatfoot,

so you'd better keep him on his toes —
I swear, I didn't mean to bring

the Bad Man into this! We should
be having fun! But I guess it shows

he's a sneaky one and tough to boot.
Get outta my story, Devil — scoot!

THE DREAM OF A MOUNTAIN WOMAN
BIG ENOUGH FOR ME

I had a pretty good'un last night,
a dream. I'm calling it The Dream

of a Mountain Woman Big Enough
for Me, a heavy title, I know,

but I like a little bigger woman,
and mountain women are something else,

because they're from the mountains, and big!
Well, anyway, in the dream I told

her everything. I told her, I like
the things that come into the world

already made, like a birdsong or
the purple on a pokeweed stem,

the humble things that humble all
the rest. You take the wind that slips

across the hill — nobody made it,
nobody taught it how to blow!

I'm telling you I like a wind!
My arms were stuck out like a scarecrow's.

She squinted her eyes and nodded slow,
then she stared right through me, smiled, and said,

You couldn't never tell me enough —
It was almost a whisper, more breath than sound,

and I knew exactly what she meant —
she wanted me to hush; so I hushed

my foolish talk and dropped my arms,
but accidentally I brushed my hand

against her leg and somehow it
got stuck, and neither of us knew

what caused it or why we couldn't get
unstuck, so I started singing that song,

the thighbone's connected to the — I paused —
the Lord. The what? she said. The Lord

told me to make you happy. Well,
she said, well ain't that somethin' — 'spose

you connect yore hand-bone to my back.
Now, words like that will fill a man

with hope. I told you mountain women
are something else, you never know,

not even in a poor man's dream
that doesn't get too far — my hand

was inches from her back and creeping
closer when I woke up. If the dream

had lasted longer, though, she had
one heck of a question to ask of me —

And did you tell the Lord you would?
She would have breathed it out like that,

our faces almost touching. If
the dream had ended there, before

I had a chance to answer? Lord knows
if I'd ever want another dream.

WHERE SADNESS COMES FROM

Don't go back to say it came from way
back when. It did, it did; but now.

When you said *did* just now, did you feel
a little dip, a curtsy in

the middle of the word, almost
another syllable but

not quite? We like to say a word,
a single word can make us feel.

There, there it is again, this time
a falling down at the end of *feel*.

You feel it, how that little sound
goes dropping down and hangs alone.

I'm here to tell you I come from
a place where hanging used to happen:

it happened in the trees, by God,
it happens even now in air,

the air the mouth lets loose; I hear
a hanging all the time. It leaves

a sadness in the voice; we speak,
and wait for history to catch up

with us. It's slow, but then, that lets
you hear it coming; you hear it now

before you speak, that sadness in
your voice, the part of you that wants

to last, to hang or dip, to hold
the word for just a little more —

my people, this is an elegy
for you, the sadness in your voice.

GIDDYUP, YE BANTIES!

What have we been talking about?
Let's see, chickens and trees, the way

the mind and what survives the mind —
I'll call it the mind gone looking for

itself in something else — the way
those two are like a horse, a horse

whose shadow goes before it, which means
the sun is up behind our friend

the horse, whose shadow walks ahead
to spook the uphill path in the pasture

and clear the way. Because at the top
of the hill is a certain persimmon tree

and it's time for those persimmons to drop.
Now that reminds me of a man

my father knew who, quote, could play
the hell out of the banjo. He sang

a tune my father sang to me:
a raccoon up in a 'simmon tree,

a possum on the ground,
the possum said, You son of a bitch,

shake them 'simmons down.
It made my father laugh to sing it.

It made me wonder if it was so,
that hell was hiding in the banjo

and the player had to pluck it out.
That's what we've been talking about,

how to pluck the hell out of the heart,
and how the hell-free heart can teach

the mind to think about chickens
or horses saddled with a shadow.

Here's the deal on all of this, pardner —
you keep the horse, if I can keep

his shadow and that persimmon tree.
We'll get the hell shook out of us

one of these days; we'll climb that hill
some morning come persimmon time,

and taste the catgut twang on our tongue
of something sour turning sweet.

THE COMMON MAN

Well, it's me, this time; I'm sitting here
in a farmhouse. Things have happened here,

besides the sun and chimney smoke,
but most of the time it's pretty quiet.

In the cemetery down the lane
there's a stone for a long-gone woman named

America, wife of so-and-so;
another woman's maiden name

was Silvertooth. Both women died
two hundred years ago. The lane

ran through the stream back then and I've found
one half of a rusty bit to prove it.

I suppose I'm common enough. I come
from this dirt, from dark Kentucky ground

steeped in blood and steep beneath
my feet. All my life, it's always up

and down. I know the lay of the land,
and like any rude provincial man,

I am content with what I know.
I know to find the yellow bar

of moonlight pouring like a soul
from the gap between two shrunken boards

of the barn, a soul beyond the body
and not inside it. Part of me

resides out there, and part of you
is out there, too. Let's hope we've got

that much in common, a fair amount
if you think about it very long.

That's something to ponder, thinking long,
not hard or deep, but long, in time

and distance — I do it all the time,
though slowly, and, as you can see,

I haven't gotten very far!
Aw shucks, I've barely ever left

the county, hardly gone beyond
the hill, because I like it here.

This morning, I took my pocketknife
and ate a turnip like an apple,

as raw as love, and right out of the ground.
It doesn't get more commonplace

than that, the dirt and bitterness
undone by a single purple curl

from the blade I sharpen Sunday nights
to keep it ready for the week.

Then I watched the horse's withers bristle;
I saw the finger of the branch

reach out to find the wind; I heard
the bird who never lets me see her —

she was telling me hello, and all
I did was whistle back, like that—

my dog ran circles around it all,
the briars bounced with joy as he weaved

his song and being through them. And then
the moon came up and I went out

to see it for a while. And that's
the way things are, a story here

and there, but mostly here. There's hope
in a world that's slowly happening,

according to its own design,
if you want to call it that. Oh, yes,

there's sorrow here, not a day goes by
that isn't stabbed with common sorrow,

with death, regret, and loneliness,
and some of us get a bigger portion

of the little tragedies. That's not
uncommon, though, now is it?

I've had my share and I'll have more,
and so will you. What matters most

is not so much what happened once,
but what will happen next. Who knows?

And then the moon rose up behind
the barn and I went out to see it.

And then I went to sleep, and then
I dreamed, and in my dream I saw

a red light tumble like a leaf
through the sky; in the morning something else

was going to happen, I knew it, but
I knew I didn't know it yet.

ACKNOWLEDGMENTS

Grateful acknowledgment is made to the following journals and magazines where some of these poems first appeared: *Appalachian Heritage, Appalachian Journal, Bat City Review, Cortland Review, Lyric, Melee, Smartish Pace, Ploughshares, Poetry, Prairie Schooner,* and *Wind.* Some of these poems were first published in a limited edition chapbook, *A Primer for the Apprehension of Heaven,* handmade by Gray Zeitz and Leslie Shane at Larkspur Press, Monterey, Kentucky.

While working on this book, I've been fortunate to receive the guidance and generosity of many friends. I would like to thank the folks at Houghton Mifflin Harcourt, in particular Jenna Johnson for continuing support and Michael Collier for laying down the law with kindness. I would also like to thank the students and faculty at Warren Wilson, especially Ellen Bryant Voigt and Peter Turchi; Kentuckians for the Commonwealth; the Whiskey Poets; and Suzanne Wise.

Finally, I must thank the good people who gather at the forks of Troublesome Creek for their fellowship and affection.